The Fish

words by Joelie Croser
illustrated by Declan Lee

"I like the sun,"
said the fish.

"I like the sun,"
said the cat.

"I like the moon,"
said the fish.

"I like the moon,"
said the cat.

"I like the stars,"
said the fish.

"I like the stars,"
said the cat.

"I like the flowers,"
said the fish.

"I like the flowers,"
said the cat.

"I like the rocks,"
said the fish.

"I like the rocks,"
said the cat.

"I like fish," said the cat.

"I like water,"
said the fish.

Splash!

"I do not like water,"
said the cat.